Guided by Stars

Roger Sipe

✹ Smithsonian

Contributing Author

Allison Duarte

Consultants

Douglas Herman, Ph.D.
Senior Geographer
National Museum of the
American Indian

Andrew Johnston, Ph.D.
Geographer
Center for Earth and Planetary
Studies
National Air and Space Museum

**Stephanie Anastasopoulos,
M.Ed.**
TOSA, STREAM Integration
Solana Beach School District

Publishing Credits

Rachelle Cracchiolo, M.S.Ed., *Publisher*
Conni Medina, M.A.Ed., *Managing Editor*
Diana Kenney, M.A.Ed., NBCT, *Content Director*
Véronique Bos, *Creative Director*
Robin Erickson, *Art Director*
Michelle Jovin, M.A., *Associate Editor*
Mindy Duits, *Senior Graphic Designer*
Smithsonian Science Education Center

Image Credits: front cover, p.1, p.25 (bottom) Herbert Kane/National
Geographic; p.7 (bottom) Courtesy Herbert K. Kane, LLC.; p.8 (bottom)
David Olsen/Alamy; p.10 (left), p.31 © Smithsonian; p.10 (right) Florilegius/
Alamy; p.11 (top) De Agostini Picture Library/Getty Images; p.13 (bottom)
Mark and Carolyn Blackburn Collection of Polynesian Art/Bridgeman
Images; p.15 (compass) Fabiola Sepulveda; p.19 (insert) Lebrecht Music
and Arts Photo Library/Alamy; p.20 (bottom) Chronicle/Alamy; p.22 (top)
Phil Uhl; p.22 (bottom) Image courtesy Jacques Descloitres, MODIS Land
Rapid Response Team at NASA GSFC; p.23 (bottom) Anders Ryman/Getty
Images; p.24 Courtesy Eddie Aikau Foundation; p.25 (top) Robert Cravens/
Shutterstock; p.27 NASA; all other images from iStock and/or Shutterstock.

Library of Congress Cataloging-in-Publication Data

Names: Sipe, Roger, author.
Title: Guided by stars / Roger Sipe.
Description: Huntington Beach, CA : Teacher Created Materials, Inc., [2019] |
   Includes index. | Audience: Grades 4 to 6. |
Identifiers: LCCN 2018018120 (print) | LCCN 2018033884 (ebook) | ISBN
   9781493869589 (E-book) | ISBN 9781493867189 (pbk.)
Subjects: LCSH: Navigation--Polynesia--Juvenile literature. |
   Polynesians--Navigation--Juvenile literature. | Nautical
   astronomy--Juvenile literature. | Stars--Navigation--Juvenile literature.
   | LCGFT: Instructional and educational works.
Classification: LCC GN440 (ebook) | LCC GN440 .S56 2019 (print) | DDC
   623.890996--dc23
LC record available at https://lccn.loc.gov/2018018120

Teacher Created Materials

5301 Oceanus Drive
Huntington Beach, CA 92649-1030
www.tcmpub.com
ISBN 978-1-4938-6718-9
© 2019 Teacher Created Materials, Inc.

Table of Contents

Oceanic Explorers

The Pacific Ocean is a huge body of water. It covers nearly one-third of Earth's surface. It is so large that all the land in the world could fit into its area.

Within this large ocean there are more than 25,000 islands. Hundreds of kilometers separate many of them. Despite the vast distances, the people of this region—Oceania—sailed these waters for more than a thousand years. They discovered every island and settled the major ones.

One group, the Polynesians, traveled the farthest. They settled what we call Polynesia. This triangle extends from the Hawaiian Islands in the north to New Zealand in the southwest. The eastern point of the triangle was Rapa Nui (RAH-puh NOO-ee), or Easter Island. Some of the world's most incredible **mariners** sailed within the triangular region's boundaries.

You might ask: How did these ancient sailors travel such extreme distances? How did they know where they were going? Didn't they have smartphones, satellites, or even magnetic compasses to guide them?

You are not the only person with those questions. Early British explorers had questions as well. When they first came in their large sailing ships to Hawai'i in the late 1700s, they were amazed at what the Polynesians had accomplished. You will be too!

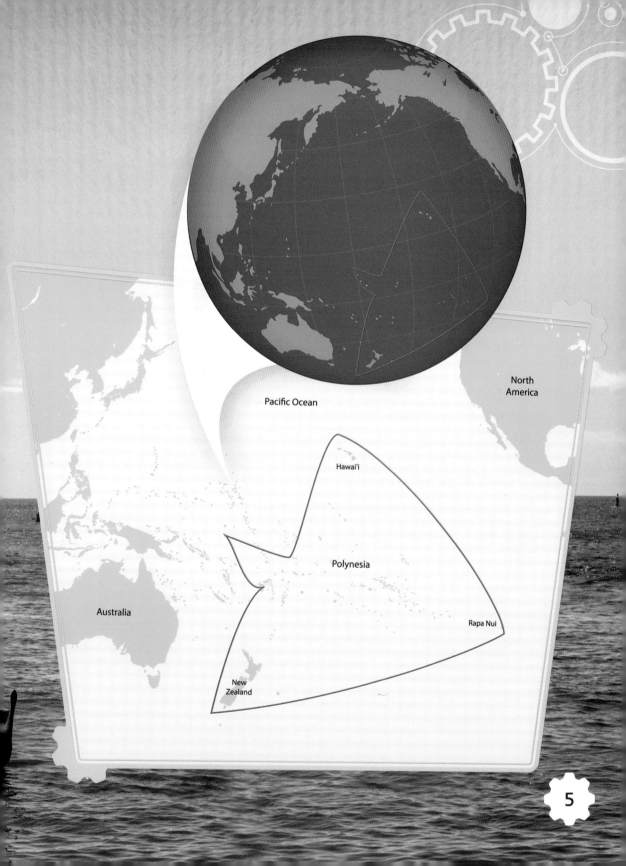

Pacific Ocean

North America

Hawai'i

Polynesia

Rapa Nui

Australia

New Zealand

Journey Preparation

Before these ancient travelers could find their way, they had to have a reason to go. They also needed a means of transportation and had to pack certain **provisions** for the long trip.

A Mighty Migration

It began a few thousand years ago. Ancient people of Southeast Asia began to take to the ocean. In time, they moved down the nearby islands and developed new cultures and languages. They did so for many reasons.

Some people left because their homes were getting overcrowded. This meant they were using more and more of their natural resources, such as land, water, and food. Some people left so they could settle new lands. And some people left just for the thrill of adventure.

It was not just men who journeyed. Whole families, including babies and grandparents, made the trips. Many passages took a day or two. But some took weeks or months. One of the greatest trips was to Hawai'i. The ancient Polynesians traveled more than 3,700 kilometers (2,300 miles) from the Marquesas Islands to get there. Whatever their reasons, once they decided to travel, they had to build seaworthy vessels.

There are more than 600 stone heads on Rapa Nui that stand about 4 meters (13 feet) tall and weigh 12.7 metric tons (14 tons). No one knows how they were built, and some have full bodies buried under hundreds of years of dirt!

partially carved Polynesian canoe

This painting shows ancient people carving a canoe and bowl.

In 1972, the remains of a canoe shed was found after having been buried for over a thousand years.

single-hulled sailing canoe with an outrigger

sail

hull

outrigger

Achieving Balance

Polynesians needed boats that would not tip over in rough surf. To solve this problem, they designed, built, and attached outriggers to their single-hulled canoes. The outrigger is made of booms and a float. The booms held the float, which acted as a counterbalance to steady the canoe.

A New Canoe

Although people still paddle single outrigger canoes, these classic canoes were not used for deep-ocean trips. Instead, ancient builders had to construct double-hulled outriggers to be powered by the wind.

Some of these boats were more than 30 m (100 ft.) long. They could carry as many as three hundred passengers. With the right wind, they could travel more than 160 km (100 mi.) each day. A small canoe might take a year to build. The larger double-hulled canoes took even longer.

Polynesians built a special shed for building their boats. To build their boats, they first ground down stone adzes, until they were sharp and tied them to handles. Then, they cut down special trees. They used the adzes to dig out hulls from the tree trunks. To raise the sides, they sewed planks together using strong rope made from coconut fibers. Workers filled the cracks between the planks with soft, green coconut fibers and breadfruit sap. They painted the boats with a mixture of saps and ashes to waterproof them.

Crossbeams connected the two hulls, and a deck was mounted in between. In the middle, workers built a small shelter as protection from any bad weather the sailors might encounter. The boats may have had one or two sails, typically made from pandanus (pan-DAH-nuhs) matting. They were steered with a single oar in the back.

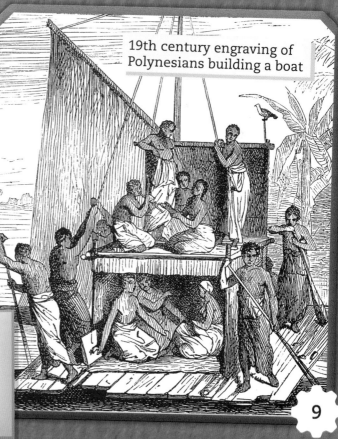

19th century engraving of Polynesians building a boat

In 1977, the first Polynesian voyaging canoe was uncovered by modern people on Huahine island in Tahiti. Before this discovery, modern people only knew about the canoes through legends.

9

What to Bring

Living in a warm climate, the Polynesians did not need to take suitcases of clothes. They wore **loincloths**, capes, and skirts made from the inner bark of paper mulberry trees. They also took mats for sleeping and sitting, tools for repairing the canoes, extra rope, and fishing gear.

The land and sea provided the travelers with everything they needed to survive on their journey. Before they set sail, they dried and **fermented** food, making it last longer. Fresh food was gathered and eaten at the start of the trip. This included breadfruit, yams, bananas, taro, sugarcane, and pandanus flour. Coconuts were also important. They provided a source of water as well as food. Fishing could be done along the way too.

Seawater is full of salt, so the voyagers couldn't drink it. Fresh water was brought aboard using natural containers, such as stalks of bamboo. Much of their water, however, would come from captured rainwater.

To survive in their new **locales** (loh-KALZ), the Polynesians had to bring their own plants as seedlings. They would plant them as soon as they landed. Pigs, chickens, and dogs were brought as **breeding stock**. That way, they would have plenty of animals in their new land.

cloths made from paper mulberry bark

Polynesian man wearing a loincloth

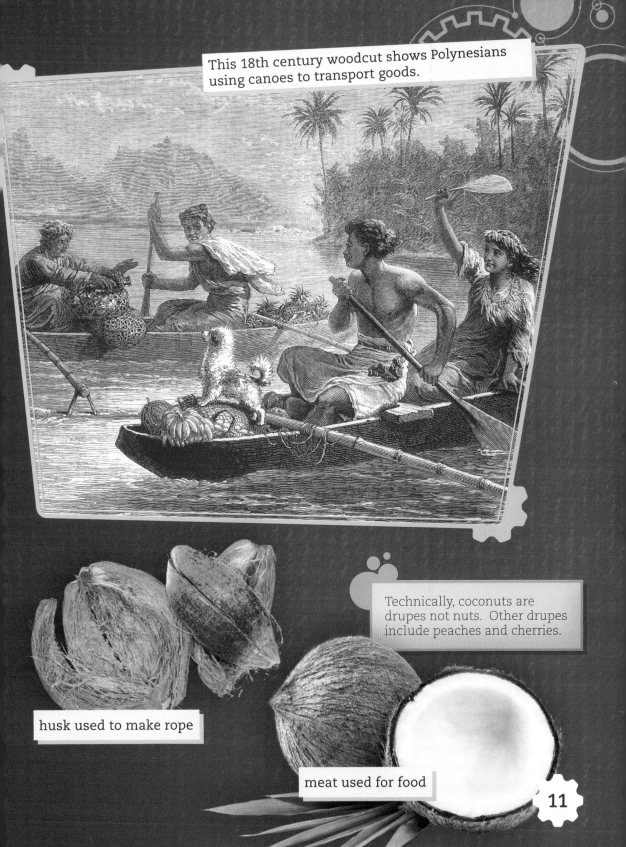

This 18th century woodcut shows Polynesians using canoes to transport goods.

Technically, coconuts are drupes not nuts. Other drupes include peaches and cherries.

husk used to make rope

meat used for food

Of Stars & Skies

If you have the opportunity, take a look at the night sky far away from city lights. There are thousands of stars and constellations to see. There are even a few visible planets, as well as Earth's moon. While we might be stargazing for fun, the ancient Polynesians saw stars as a road map.

Our Brightest Star

There is one star visible during the day: the sun. Every 24 hours, Earth makes one rotation. Every day, the rotation causes the sun to rise in the east and set in the west.

In the middle of the ocean on a clear day, finding which direction a mariner was going was easy. Twice a day, navigators knew which direction they were headed. In the morning, the rising sun pointed east. They knew that the opposite direction was west. They could then determine which ways were north and south. At dusk, they knew that the setting sun pointed west and could confirm the other directions, as they did in the morning.

When the sun sets or rises on the Pacific Ocean's horizon, there is sometimes a green flash. The rare color appears from bending light caused by Earth's atmosphere.

People gaze at an outline of the Kā Hei-hei o Na Keiki (Orion) constellation.

Polynesian navigators adjusted the path of their canoes according to the sun.

Night Lights

Ancient navigators used many stars to keep a proper heading at night. As Earth turns, stars parade across the night sky, rising on the eastern horizon. Navigators could determine from their locations which way their canoes were heading.

Back then, there weren't computers that navigators could use to look up the quickest routes. Instead, they pictured maps in their heads. They saw the rising and setting points of the nighttime stars and constellations.

Navigators learned the paths of many, many stars: where they rose and where they set. Unless a person is at the equator, the tilt of Earth means those star paths are on an angle. So each star is only useful for direction when it is near the horizon. Because the night sky shifts over the course of the year, navigators had to be familiar with the entire sky.

Some stars appear to pass directly over an island when a canoe is due east or west. They are called zenith stars. Hōkūle'a, or Arcturus, is the zenith star for Hawai'i. When navigators saw that star, they knew they were on the right track.

Constellations' positions changed as canoes got closer to the equator. Good navigators adjusted for those changes. They could also adjust for unforeseen issues, such as clouds or stormy skies.

There are more than a hundred billion stars in the Milky Way galaxy.

'ĀKAU
North

Haka · Nā Leo · Nālani · Manu · Noio · 'Āina · Lā

HO'OLUA
Northwest

KO'OLAU
Northeast

KOMOHANA
West

HIKINA
East

Lā · 'Āina

KONA
Southwest

MALANAI
Southeast

Noio · Manu · Nālani · Nā Leo · Haka

HEMA
South

Modern navigators use
star compasses to find
which direction they
are heading.

North & South

Tahiti is south of the equator; Hawai'i is north of it. When voyagers in the South started on their trips, they relied on Hanaiakamalama (the Southern Cross) for help. In the night sky, the five stars of the Southern Cross look like a kite. The top and bottom stars form a line pointing south. If a navigator was headed north toward Hawai'i, these stars appeared to be moving lower in the sky.

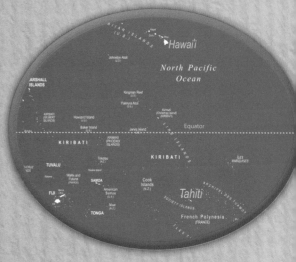

The Southern Cross is only visible in the Southern Hemisphere. Luckily, there is a star that helped navigators after they crossed the equator: Hokupa'a (the North Star). The North Star does not rise or set. It is always in the same location in the sky. Navigators used the North Star to find the rest of their way to Hawai'i.

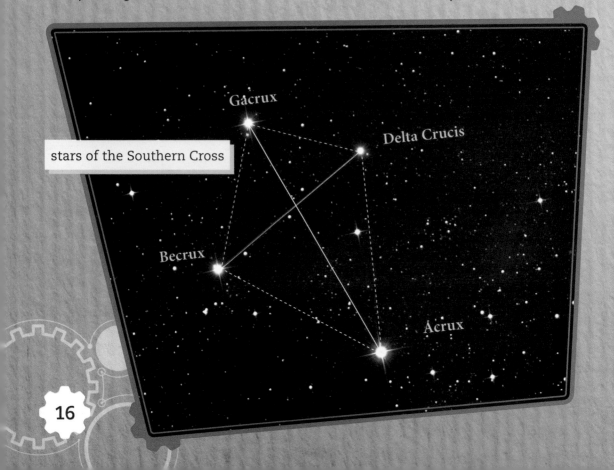

stars of the Southern Cross

Gacrux

Delta Crucis

Becrux

Ácrux

phases of the moon

Moon & Planets

Like the sun, the moon rises and sets each day. Navigators used it for direction, as well as to track the passage of time. Hawaiians created a calendar based on the different phases of the moon, which repeats roughly every 30 days.

Depending on the time of year, some planets could be seen in the sky. In Hawaiian, they are called *hōkū 'ae'a*, meaning, "traveling (or wandering) stars." Their rising and setting points can be determined from nearby stars. Of the eight planets in our solar system, Hawaiians—without the aid of telescopes—knew five.

MATHEMATICS

Going the Distance

Multiply speed by time traveled to find distance traveled. For instance, if you travel 8 km (5 mi.) per hour for 2 hours, you will have moved 16 km (10 mi.). Early navigators knew how many days it took to travel between islands. They also tracked stars, wind patterns, and waves. Then, they could mentally track speed and elapsed time to calculate distance.

Of Wind & Waves

During the day or on cloudy nights, the stars are of no use. Ancient seafarers realized they could steer by **swells**. Swells are crisscrossing patterns of waves that regularly move across the ocean. Once a navigator had set a course, they would feel how the swells rocked the canoe. Navigators were trained from childhood to be sensitive to this feeling. They could hold their canoes on course by keeping that rhythm. If the motions changed, they knew their canoes were off track.

One group of people from Oceania was the Micronesians. They identified eight different sets of swells coming from eight different directions. They trained in how to recognize them by sight and feel.

Oceanian navigators also had to account for ocean currents. They had to know how wind would push their canoes sideways. They would change the directions of their canoes to counter these effects.

Navigators had to keep track of distance on top of everything else. The sea may look like a flat, featureless expanse of blue. But navigators knew how to mark distances in their heads. They used speed and time of travel to find the distances they had traveled. This knowledge came from years of training and experience.

TECHNOLOGY

Map Quest

Ancient navigators did not have traditional compasses, GPS, or map apps to guide them. They did, however, take all that they learned from waves and create what are known today as stick charts. These charts were made from wood (such as bamboo) coconut fiber, and shells. Shells indicated islands, and curved pieces of wood showed how waves acted around islands.

stick chart

Navigators exploring the oceans did not know what was out there. The curvature of Earth kept them from seeing very far. So they had to learn methods for "seeing" land past the horizon. They learned a few signs.

The first sign of land was clouds that weren't moving. An island of any height forces wind to go up and form clouds. While other clouds on the horizon will move, these clouds tend to stay over the island.

The second sign was the color on the undersides of clouds. Bright clouds might mean there was sand below, as light reflected back up. Dark clouds might mean there were lots of trees below. But these colors are very **subtle**. Again, it took years of training and experience to detect these colors.

The third sign of land was birds. Some birds do not fly far from land. White and noddy terns were important navigational aids. Both birds fly to the sea in the morning and return to their nests at dusk. White terns can fly over 190 km (120 mi.) from land. Noddy terns only range about 65 km (40 mi.) from land. Wise navigators followed these birds to shore.

Navigators could also check the ocean for swell patterns and floating debris, known as flotsam. These palm **fronds**, coconuts, and other types of vegetation signaled that land was nearby.

This 19th century engraving shows Polynesian voyagers steering a double-hulled canoe.

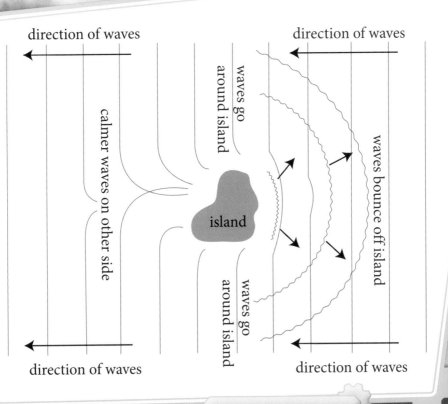

direction of waves

direction of waves

waves go around island

calmer waves on other side

waves bounce off island

island

waves go around island

direction of waves

direction of waves

The Science of Swells

When a swell hits an island, it wraps around and causes lines of waves on the other side. Some of the swell also bounces back, causing lines of waves on the front side. Navigators could use these lines to find land. Skilled navigators could read these wave lines from up to 72 km (45 mi.) away from the island.

arrival of the Hōkūle'a in 1976

The Hawaiian Islands are made up of eight major islands and stretch for more than 2,400 km (1,500 mi.).

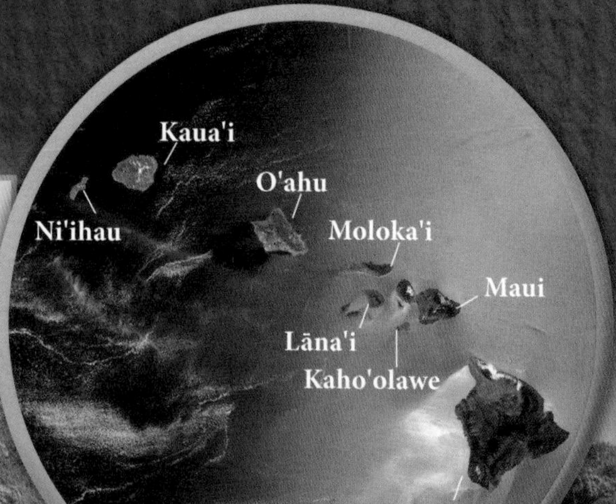

Kaua'i

Ni'ihau

O'ahu

Moloka'i

Maui

Lāna'i

Kaho'olawe

Hawai'i

Keepers of Culture

Long-distance voyages stopped about six hundred years ago. No one is sure why that happened. By the time Western explorers arrived, very few large canoes were left.

A Voyage of Rediscovery

Native Hawaiians were rediscovering their culture in the 1970s. They were recovering their native language, their history, and their arts. A small group even looked toward the ocean. They formed the Polynesian Voyaging Society and set a course for discovery.

The goal was to travel to Tahiti without technology. They wanted to prove their ancestors had purposely sailed to the islands. Some historians claimed the ancients had found the islands by accident while lost at sea. So this group built a double-hulled canoe and named it *Hōkūle'a*, after Hawai'i's zenith star.

They had one problem: none of them knew how to navigate like their ancestors. But there was a man willing to teach them. Mau Piailug (MOW pee-AHY-luhg) lived on an island thousands of kilometers away. His grandfather was a master navigator and had handed down his knowledge. He was Hawaiian society's best hope.

In 1976, the first crew of the *Hōkūle'a* left Hawai'i for Tahiti. Piailug guided the boat using only the ancient techniques. After more than a month, the boat arrived to a blissful crowd of Tahitians. They had done it!

Mau Piailug teaches his son and grandson how to navigate using a star compass.

Master Sailors

In 1978, the society set sail again. This time, they traveled without Piailug. However, a storm capsized the boat. Crewmember Eddie Aikau paddled away on his surfboard to get help. He was never seen again. The crew was eventually rescued, but they were heartbroken at the loss of their friend. Instead of giving up, they carried on to fulfill his dreams.

In 1979, Piailug trained Nainoa (nigh-NOH-uh) Thompson to become a master navigator. Thompson learned from his teacher how to read the stars and the waves. In 1980, he launched a successful second voyage to Tahiti and back. He was the first Hawaiian to do so in more than six hundred years.

For the next several decades, the society continued to sail the ocean. Crews met with people from Alaska to Japan. They created programs for schools. They inspired others to build canoes. They also built another canoe themselves.

In 2014, the society set sail around the world. Its goal this time was to "chart a positive course for our planet." The crew met with communities and talked to them about how to live sustainably. They returned to Hawai'i three years later.

Eddie Aikau was a big-wave surfer. Each year, a surfing tournament is held in honor of Aikau when waves are at least 6 m (20 ft.) tall!

Nainoa Thompson

Drawing Inspiration

Herb Kane was an artist and a historian. He painted hundreds of scenes of ancient Hawai'i. However, his greatest work of art was the Hōkūle'a. First, he created detailed drawings. Then, crewmembers used that painting to construct a seaworthy voyaging canoe.

painting by Herb Kane

Beyond the Sea

Polynesian voyages did not always end peacefully. Many people were lost to the ocean. It required a lot of planning and nice weather to safely reach an island. More importantly, it took a master navigator.

Those navigators had to be brave. They also had to be experts at their craft. They had to continue studying and learning their whole lives. Navigators had to memorize the positions of many stars. They had to know the birds of the sky and the animals in the sea. They sometimes had to literally feel their way across the ocean. Their lives and their crewmembers' lives depended on it.

Today, oceans have been mapped and charted. Ships routinely sail between Hawai'i and other islands and continents. Modern explorers still look to the sky, though. They now want to explore space. Hawai'i has been the birthplace of two astronauts. Maybe one day, a **descendant** of navigators will chart a course to a new planet. And none of that would be possible without the brave voyagers who took to the seas hundreds of years ago.

part of the Mauna Kea Observatories in Hawai'i

One of Hawai'i's astronauts was Ellison Shoji Onizuka. He was the first Asian American and the first person of Japanese descent to go into space.

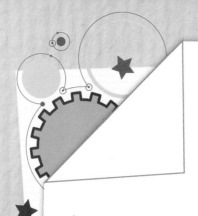

STEAM CHALLENGE

Define the Problem

Ancient Polynesians designed outrigger canoes that allowed them to explore the vast ocean around them. They were successful because the canoes were stable in the water and used wind power to move. Your task is to build a model of an outrigger canoe that is both stable in the water and powered by wind.

Constraints: Your canoe must be made out of at least one material found in nature.

Criteria: Build a small model of an outrigger canoe that floats and moves across the water without tipping over when it is blown by wind.

Research and Brainstorm

1

How did ancient navigators design and build outrigger canoes? How was wind power used? What types of navigational information can wind provide? Will your canoe have sails? Will it be a single-hulled or double-hulled canoe?

Design and Build

2

Sketch your design of the canoe. What purpose does each part serve? What materials will work best? Collect materials and build the model.

Test and Improve

3

Test your canoe by placing it in a large basin filled with water. Use a fan to act as wind. Does the canoe float? Does it move without tipping over? How can it be improved? Modify your design and try again.

Reflect and Share

4

Can you build an outrigger canoe using fewer materials? Can you design a different model? Can you think of another way to test your canoe?

Glossary

adzes—cutting tools with thin blades used for shaping wood

breadfruit sap—a sticky liquid that comes from a round fruit, which resembles bread in color and texture when baked

breeding stock—a group of animals used to have babies to build a herd

capsized—overturned

constellations—groups of stars that form shapes in the sky and have been given names

crossbeams—pieces of wood that go across boats' frames for strength

descendant—an offspring in a family's direct line, such as a child

fermented—caused a chemical reaction in food

fronds—large leaves of a palm tree

hulls—frames or bodies of ships

locales—places

loincloths—pieces of cloth worn around the hips

mariners—people who work on or control boats with sails

outrigger—a frame that extends from a boat's side to prevent it from flipping over

pandanus—a tropical tree with long, spiny leaves

provisions—supplies of food and other needed things

subtle—hard to notice; not obvious

sustainably—using methods that do not completely use up or destroy natural resources

swells—long rolling waves or a series of waves in the ocean

Index

Do you want to be a master navigator?
Here are some tips to get you started.

"Learn the stars. You don't need to be an astronomer or have a telescope to learn the constellations. Watch the night sky, and use a guide (an app, even) to learn as much as you can. When you can glance up at the night sky and immediately recognize what you are seeing, you are way ahead of the game." —*Andrew Johnston, Geographer*

"Spend as much time in boats as you can. The more familiar you are with how boats work and how the ocean behaves, the more ready you are to learn navigation. Even if you start out on a pond, lake, or river, you are learning to handle a boat and all the skills involved." —*Douglas Herman, Senior Geographer*